There Is
A WORD FOR
EVERY STORM!

*How to Overcome the Storms of Life
with One Word from God*

By Kathy Casto

Hisway
Prayer Publication
P.O. Box 762
Jamul, CA 91935

There is a Word for Every Storm

How to Overcome the Storms of Life with One Word from God

ISBN-978-1-879545-04-5

Copyright © 2019 by Kathy Casto

All rights reserved

Printed in the United States of America

Published by Hisway Prayer Publications

P. O. Box 762

Jamul, CA 91935

Dedication

To my loving husband who has been
my encouragement
& best friend through all the storms of life –

Together we became strong!

Foreword

For twenty years, Kathy Casto has faithfully served on my staff. During that time, I, my family, and staff have learned to respect how seriously she takes prayer. We also value the dynamic way that, by focusing her prayers on the Word of God, actual, meaningful, tangible results are achieved in peoples' lives.

As you begin this journey with her, open your heart and expect God to take you to a new level as an intercessor.

Dr. Morris Cerullo, President

Morris Cerullo World Evangelism

Table of Contents

The Strength Within

"I'm never down…I'm either up or I'm getting up."[1]

I discovered the above quote from John Ortberg in one of my devotional books recently and recognized it as the theme of my life now. Unfortunately, in my earlier years of marriage (teens and twenties), I struggled through the challenges of life, not knowing how to deal with them. It was easy to become overwhelmed, distressed, and sometimes hopeless. However, I found the answer. I learned there is a Word (scripture) for every storm in life – a specific Word for a specific problem. As I became proficient in wielding the sword of the Spirit, I developed an amazing strength within. The chapter of faith found in Hebrews 11:34 proved to be true: *"whose weakness turned to strength; and who became powerful in battle and routed foreign armies"* (NIV).

It would be wonderful to live an idyllic life with no troubles, stress, sickness or conflicts; however, we do not live in a perfect world. We live in a fallen world. Scripture says, *"In this world you will have trouble"* (John 16:33, NIV). However, I have good news. Although we live in this world of trouble, we can rise above the trouble, or even better, make trouble run from us. We do not have to accept the storms that blow into our lives, toss us around, and try to destroy our homes, families, health, businesses or jobs.

Are you hopeless, distressed, depressed or completely overwhelmed? If so you can find your strength in the power of the Spirit of God who resides within. With just a simple decision of repentance, you can go through life with the Creator of the universe leading and guiding you as you train yourself to hear by the Spirit.

In the following chapters, we will learn to see through the storm, speak to the storm, walk out of the storm and at times, stand still in the storm. In every case, we will overcome because *"Greater is He that is within us than he that is in the world"* (John 4:4, NIV).

Notes:

1. Gass, Bob *The Word for You Today* p 16.

Chapter One
The Storms Within

"Storms in life are not an option;
we must simply learn to fight."

What is a storm and how do we recognize we are in one? A "storm" is a crisis, challenge or anything in our lives we perceive as threatening or dangerous. I chose the analogy of storms to paint a word picture of how the challenging circumstances of life make us feel at times. Each bad report, hurtful word, financial crisis or physical ailment can toss us to and fro in life's horrible storms.

A storm is defined as 1) A violent disturbance of the atmosphere with strong winds and usually rain thunder, lighting, or snow 2) A tumultuous reaction; an uproar or controversy or 3) A direct assault by troops on a fortified place.[2] These definitions depict exactly how we feel at times as the storms of life affect our emotions and mental state causing physical breakdowns.

We find ourselves in troubling situations that are as threatening as the tumultuous winds. Overwhelming problems with our children, health or work buffet us. Like the frightening thunder and lightning in a thunderstorm or tornado, the problems scream at us drowning out reason or the calming voice of peace. Controversy stirs up when voices of accusation play over and over in our minds — whether they are true or false. The accusations batter our minds; they frustrate us and create panic. It seems when one challenge is solved another emerges, similar to the third definition stated above of troops assaulting a hill with wave after wave of battalions determined to conquer.

Let's consider storms for a moment. There are many types of storms across our nation. Depending on where we live, the storms have different magnitudes, patterns, and levels of destruction. Growing up in Arkansas, we lived in what is called "Tornado Alley" consisting of the states most frequented by tornadoes: Oklahoma, Kansas, Arkansas, Texas, Louisiana, etc. During the five years my husband and I lived on the East Coast, we were terrorized by hurricanes. Now we live in California, and firestorms threaten our homes every fall, which is "fire season." The threat of all these natural disasters can easily cause us to live in fear of loss, worry, anxiety, and at times debilitating panic as the storms' battering seems incessant.

Notice the storms I referred to are called "natural disasters" – tornadoes, hurricanes, firestorms, as well as ice storms, and blizzards. They occur in the natural or physical world where our senses are barraged.

Just as the natural weather storms affect our natural senses and emotions, the challenges of life we have labeled as storms affect us on many different levels: physical, mental, emotional, and spiritual. They can rob us of our peace and joy; they can also send us into depression emotionally and mentally. The emotional stress from the storms of life can cause physical illnesses. These storms may be created by family or other close relationship problems, financial or business issues, as well as threatening circumstances affecting our visions or purposes in life.

We have briefly examined the ferocity of storms and natural disasters in our physical world. However, we will shift our attention and focus on a different world. Our problems must be addressed from a perspective other than that of the natural or physical world. We will learn to address them in the realm of the spirit.

Dr. Morris Cerullo teaches, "All truth is parallel."[2] He is a great Bible teacher and world-renowned missionary evangelist for 75 years as of this writing. Dr. Cerullo emphasizes that whatever happens in the spirit world creates a reaction in the natural world. And whatever happens in the natural world creates a reaction in the spirit world. This is discussed more fully in the following chapters.

As the years pass, it may seem as if when one storm dissipates, another is on the horizon. An excellent Bible teacher once said, "You will never outgrow warfare...you must simply learn to fight."[3] I would like to rephrase it for this study, "Challenges in life (storms) are not an option, and we must simply learn to fight." So let's get to it. Remember in every case, we will overcome because *"Greater is He that is within us than he that is in the world"* (I John 4:4, NIV).

Notes:

1. Reader's Digest Oxford Complete Wordfinder p 1054.

2. Cerullo, Morris *Proof Producers: "What We Must Do to Work the Works of God"* p 335.

3. Murdock, Mike *101 Wisdom Keys* p 25.

Chapter Two
The Answer Within

"Life never gets any easier, we get stronger."[1]

The Spirit of the Lord once whispered to me, "You've got the power, now use it." I knew exactly what He meant when He spoke those words. It was time to establish a special prayer group at our church that would assault the Spirit world on behalf of others. Proverbs 31:8 became our founding scripture: *"Speak up for those who cannot speak for themselves"* (NIV).

The principles of prayer we learned from our mentor, Dr. B. J. Willhite were the principles we embraced in our lives, that we taught in our church, and what I want to share with you now to build your faith. (Dr. B. J. Willhite was an Elder and Pastor of Prayer at Church on the Rock in Rockwall, Texas. He later established the National Prayer Embassy in Washington, D.C. and the radio program,

National Call to Prayer). These principles of prayer radically changed our lives and the lives of those we taught as we crisscrossed the nation for several years. As I applied these teachings to my life, I went from being in a weak, fearful, vulnerable state – blown about by every wind of adversity – to a position of strength and power in the Spirit. Let me explain.

When those overwhelming storms first blew into our lives, they hit us in many different areas. My husband had been a youth Pastor for 12 years, had always been a strong man of prayer, and walked exuberantly with God. At this stage of our lives, he became so discouraged in ministry due to the politics within our church and turmoil between our denomination's leaders that he was depressed and questioned the ministry altogether. (This was a major divergence from the happy-go-lucky, sanguine temperament that wakes up normally singing/whistling in the mornings!) My husband, who had always been so strong spiritually, was drowning in despair. On top of that, our baby was screaming through the nights with high fevers and ear infections month after month. The doctor had no answers or cures for the illness.

With no help to be found, I did what most young mothers would do. I went home to my mom for answers. This was a difficult journey halfway across the country from Virginia to Arkansas. It may seem like no big deal these days; however, as a young woman on an extremely tight budget with two little ones under five flying alone, it was challenging to say the least. One businessman looked at me when I boarded the plane and found my seat close to him and said, "You are very brave." He was probably thinking, "Is there another seat available? Anywhere?"

The trip was to no avail, however. I had traveled home hoping for some words of wisdom or comfort from Mom; instead, I found her in a deep depression. Having a baby at age 43 plunged her into postpartum depression from which she never recovered. It was five years later, and she was still sad and discouraged. She even said she would not care if she died. She was looking to *me* for answers...help!

As I returned home, I realized it was time for me to grow up. No one I knew had any answers. The doctors, educators, and my formerly strong husband could not help me. And now, my mom was struggling. I turned to the only source I believed could help. I prayed. I told God, "I know you are the God I have heard about all my life in church. You are the God my husband has cried out to for years. Now, it is time for you to be my God. I need some answers. We need help."

As I prayed, I heard the scripture, *"Get your house in order"* (2 Kings 20:1, NIV). Every day after my husband went to work, I would hear, "Get your house in order." Of course, if you know that scripture, those are the words the prophet Isaiah spoke to King Hezekiah because he was going to die. After the king repented, the Lord healed him and gave him an additional fifteen years to live (2 Kings 20:6). Although I knew the story, I did not take it as a warning that death was looming. I knew in my spirit God was telling me to get "my house" or my family (my husband and children) in order by the Spirit. I also knew I was to pray an hour each day to accomplish this.

I confess this was a difficult challenge for me. I had never prayed more than a few minutes before I went to sleep at night. Now, I was faced with the challenge of praying for an hour for my family to "get my house in order." At that time, I had never heard of anybody praying for an hour a day consistently. I will say I was obedient and the scripture proved to be true, *"Draw near to God and He will draw near to you"* (James 4:8, NKJV).

At first, I would list all our needs and tell God what He should do to work out our problems. That took about ten minutes. Then I would force myself to stay there for the rest of the hour. Many times, I prayed in the Spirit for the remainder of the time. I kept thinking, "There must be more to prayer than this. I need more instruction...more understanding." God saw my frustration, heard the cry of my heart, and sent the answer.

My husband John knew I was struggling to pray for an hour every day although I was faithful in my attempts. He came home from work one afternoon and said, "Kathy, look what I got in the mail today!" It was an audio teaching series entitled, "Could You Not Tarry One Hour?" based on the Lord's Prayer. This was like manna from heaven to me. I eagerly listened to the teaching and applied it to my prayer time. Praying for an hour became easy. The teaching series used the Lord's Prayer as an outline and allowed me to systematically cover every area of my life in prayer: my loved ones, health, finances, etc. It truly took me to a whole new level of prayer.

I had a vision of myself as I prayed. I was a female warrior lying down on a low chaise-like sofa similar to something you would see in Roman times. The warrior attire even looked like the one worn in that era. Over the months as I continued to pray, I saw the warrior sit up and eventually, she stood up with the sword raised in one hand and the shield in the other. I knew I was that warrior, and I was learning to fight.

During this first year of prayer, I received many answers. A friend who was a nurse guided me to an extremely knowledgeable doctor who diagnosed our baby's problem as allergies and pointed us in the right direction to health and recovery. My husband realized his season was over as a youth Pastor, and God was calling him to a new assignment. The most important part of the prayer, *"Thy kingdom come, thy will be done on earth as it is in heaven"* initiated a change in the heavens that manifested in the natural realm. God's will for our lives was no longer in Virginia in youth ministry.

That same year, a commercial slogan on television depicted what we were experiencing, "The Winds of Change are Blowing." Truly, that succinct phrase was exactly what was happening in our lives. When we began to pray, *"Thy kingdom come; thy will be done in our lives, as it is in heaven,"* my husband's years serving as a youth Pastor ended. We relocated from Virginia to Texas to start a new season in our lives *in the will of God.* When you sincerely pray, *"Thy kingdom come; thy will be done in my life as it is in heaven"* – hold on!

This move was made entirely upon the prompting of the Spirit of God. We had no jobs waiting for us in Texas. We knew no one in the town of Rockwall or at the church where we planned to rest and recuperate for a couple of months. These were our plans: relocate to Texas, attend the church that was teaching "Could You Not Tarry One Hour?" and go to the prayer meetings for two or three months. Then, we would be on our way. We were sure God would open a door. The move was made on the prophetic word my husband heard while attending the Pastors' conference sponsored by this church, "Join yourself to this man. Learn of me and I will send you forth." Needless to say, our plans are not always God's plans.

"One thing I do, forget the past, press forward to what is ahead" (Philippians 3:13, NIV).

"Forget the former things; do not dwell on the past. See, I am doing a new thing! Now it springs up, do you not perceive it? I am making a way in the desert and streams in the wasteland" (Isaiah 43:18-19, NIV).

Notes:

1. Author Unknown.

Chapter Three
The Power Within

"Struggle is the proof you have not yet been conquered."[1]

When we arrived in Rockwall, Texas, my husband promptly started attending the morning prayer sessions at 5:00 a.m. and 6:00 a.m. Yes, I said 5:00 a.m. Whoever heard of early morning prayer meetings at five o'clock in the morning? I learned that this church was following the pattern of prayer and cell groups that Dr. Yonggi Cho had exemplified to the world in Seoul, South Korea. Dr. Cho attributed praying and obeying as his pattern for successful church growth. Today, the church Dr. Cho founded reports membership of 830,000. Church on the Rock in Rockwall, Texas, had experienced exponential growth, as well, and was nearing 8000 people. The church attributed its successful growth to the daily prayer sessions and the unique "care group" network that was new to the church world at that time.

At first, I stayed home with the two little ones while John went to the prayer meetings. During my devotions, I heard the Spirit of God say to me, "What kind of house will you build for me?" I was completely surprised by the question. Not really knowing the answer, I simply said, "Any kind you want." Interestingly, that same morning, John brought a tape home after the 6:00 a.m. prayer meeting for me to listen to by Dr. B. J. Willhite, the Pastor of Prayer. "Kathy, you have got to listen to this teaching. It is phenomenal!" John's excitement was contagious. The first words I heard when the teaching began were, "What kind of house will you build for the Lord? There are many kinds of houses – houses of worship, houses of teaching, houses of preaching – but Jesus said, 'My house shall be called a house of prayer'" (Matthew 21:13, NIV). I knew exactly what God was asking of me. As I became a house of prayer, our family and ministry would be a house of prayer. Acts 1:8 confirmed that revelation to me that morning: *"But you will receive power when the Holy Spirit comes on you; and you will be my witnesses in Jerusalem (represented my personal life), and in all Judea and Samaria, (the surrounding area or my close family) and to the ends of the earth (our ministry would take us across the nation and to the nations of the earth)"* (NIV).

I soon began to attend the morning prayer sessions with John. The girls would sleep on the pews during the prayer meetings and then go to school and preschool afterward. During these days, we absorbed the prayer teachings and implemented them in our lives. I realized something profound; if I did not pray for my husband, who would? If I did not pray for my children, who would? If I did not pray for my loved ones, our church, community, and nation — who would? I began to see that my prayers made a difference. Let me explain.

Divine Intervention

Through the early morning prayer teachings, I started to understand the principle of "Divine Intervention." John Wesley, the great revivalist said, "God does nothing but in answer to prayer." The second part of his statement is just as powerful: "and everything by it." Dick Eastman, a contemporary man of prayer known for his book, *The Hour That Changes the World*, explained his experiences in prayer while conducting a conference at our church, "When I pray something supernatural happens in the heavens. When I don't pray, the heavens stand still." Dr. B. J. Willhite continually taught, "If you have enough faith to pray, you have enough faith to move the hand of God."[2] As these truths sank into my spirit, I knew my prayers were very significant, strategic, and effective. For emphasis, let's look at these principles again:

17

1. "God does nothing but in answer to prayer, and everything by it" (John Wesley).

2. "Something supernatural happens in the heavens when I pray. When I don't pray, the heavens stand still." (Dick Eastman).

3. "If you have enough faith to pray, you have enough faith to move the hand of God" (Dr. B. J. Willhite).

Voice in the Land

God is looking for a "voice in the land." He will not impose His will on the earth. He is listening and watching for someone to come into agreement with His will to implement it upon the earth.

"I looked for someone among them who would build up the wall and stand before me in the gap on behalf of the land so I would not have to destroy it, but I found no one" (Ezekiel 22:30, NIV).

"Speak up for those who cannot speak for themselves, for the rights of all who are destitute. Speak up and judge fairly, defend the rights of the poor and needy (Proverbs 31:8-9, NIV).

"What is mankind that you make so much of them, that you give them so much attention, and that you examine them every morning" (Job 7:17-18, NIV)

We see from these scriptures that morning by morning, the Lord is examining the hearts of men. He is listening for a "voice in the land." God is listening for someone to cry out to Him for mercy so judgment will not fall upon our nation, loved ones, and our very lives.

God's judgment is always plan "Plan B." "Plan A" is always mercy. God longs to extend mercy. Look at the story of Noah and the flood. Even though there was only one righteous person left on the earth, God still wanted to save mankind through Noah and his family. In the book of Ezekiel, He told the prophet He looked for a man to stand in the gap for the nation, so he could extend mercy instead of judgment. In Jeremiah 18:8 this is also confirmed, *"And if that nation I warned repents of the evil, then I will relent and not inflict on it the disaster I had planned"* (NIV),

Even the patriarch Abraham, known as the friend of God, knew God's nature. When the heavenly visitors on their way to Sodom and Gomorrah came to Abraham, he knew the Lord really wanted to spare the city if He could find ten righteous men. He sought for a man (Abraham) to stand in the gap on behalf of Sodom and Gomorrah, so He would not have to destroy it, but He found none (ten righteous could not be found). Why else did the Lord say, *"Shall I hide from Abraham what I am about to do?"* (Genesis 18:17, NIV).

The Lord wanted someone to ask for mercy. He wanted a voice in the land crying out for mercy. I have determined I want to be a voice the Lord hears morning by morning crying out on behalf of my loved ones, our leaders, and those who cannot speak for themselves. Will you not also do the same? Who is crying out on behalf of your loved ones? *"Surely the Sovereign Lord does nothing without revealing his plan to his servants the prophets"* (Amos 3:7 NIV).

The Hearing Ear

The prophet Jeremiah declares, *"Call unto me and I will answer you and tell you great and unsearchable things you do not know"* (Jeremiah 33:3 NIV). Our heavenly Father wants us to call to Him; however, He also wants us to listen. He has important things He wants to share with us — great, unsearchable things we do not know He is willing to share when He finds someone He can trust. *"Before they call I will answer; while they are still speaking I will hear"* (Isaiah 65:24, NIV). Again, He is listening and waiting for us to call to Him! He wants to answer us. *"He sends his command to the earth; his word runs swiftly"* (Psalm 147:15, NIV).

God sends His commands morning by morning to us who are made from the earth. Are we listening? Do we hear the commands coming from heaven each morning? He sends His instructions and will for the day to those who are listening. He sends them to those who will hear and proclaim into the heavenlies by the words of our mouths what must be done that day. The words we speak are in agreement with His will. Why is this so important? Listen to this scripture in Psalm 103:20-21, *"Praise the Lord, you his angels, you mighty ones who do His bidding, who obey His word....who do His will."* The angels of God obey His Word. They do His will as they receive their assignments morning by morning. This is what Dick Eastman meant when he said, "When I pray something supernatural moves in the heavens. When I don't pray, the heavens stand still."

Based on these scriptures, I believe the angels of God are "voice-activated" when we proclaim the Word of God. Listen to what the angel Gabriel said to Daniel, *"From the first day that you set your mind to gain understanding and to humble yourself before your God, your words were heard, and I have come in response to them"* (Daniel 10:12, NIV; emphasis mine).

Daniel was a man of prayer. He prayed three times a day. However, this pattern of seeking God was used against him by his enemies; they wanted him dead, thrown in the lions' den to be devoured.

It is interesting that after Daniel's near-death experience, he studied the prophecies of Jeremiah, discerned that it was time for the captives to return to the land of Israel, and repented for the sins of Israel as a nation. His prayers and fasting opened the way for their release in the heavens. It manifested on the earth with their return to rebuild the temple in Jerusalem as recorded in the books of Ezra and Nehemiah.

The Enemy knows who the deliverers are and always tries to kill them (Joseph, Moses, all the baby boys at Jesus' birth by Herod), but our God is stronger! In the book of Hebrews, we see the angels are sent to help us, to work for us, and to see the will of God is accomplished in our lives. *"Are not all angels ministering spirits sent to serve those who will inherit salvation?"* (Hebrews 1:14, NIV).

Let's take an example from Acts Chapter 12. In this chapter, King Herod took Peter as a prisoner after he had James, the brother of John, killed by the sword because it pleased the Jews. Nowhere in the Bible does it mention that the church prayed for the release of James. Perhaps they all thought it was not necessary since he was one of the apostles. However, after James was killed, Peter was arrested and the trial set for the next day. In verse five, we find that the church was earnestly praying to God for him. What happened next? An angel was sent to the prison cell. He woke him up; the chains fell off his wrists and the angel led him past the two sets of guards. The iron gate opened by itself to let them through. After walking one street with Peter, the angel disappeared.

The night before Herod was to bring him to trial, Peter was sleeping between two soldiers, bound with two chains, and sentries stood guard at the entrance. Suddenly an angel of the Lord appeared and a light shone in the cell. He struck Peter on the side and woke him up. 'Quick, get up!' he said, and the chains fell off Peter's wrists.

Then the angel said to him, 'Put on your clothes and sandals.' And Peter did so. 'Wrap your cloak around you and follow me,'" the angel told him. Peter followed him out of the prison, but he had no idea that what the angel was doing was really happening; he thought he was seeing a vision They passed the first and second guards and came to the iron gate leading to the city. It opened for them by itself, and they went through it. When they had walked the length of one street, suddenly the angel left him."

Then Peter came to himself and said, 'Now I know without a doubt that the Lord sent his angel and rescued me from Herod's clutches and from everything the Jewish people were anticipating. (Acts 12:6-11, NIV)

Let me re-emphasize that when we pray, all of heaven goes to work for us. When I say, "All of heaven goes to work for us," I am referring to the angels of God. Just as they were dispatched to release Peter from prison in response to the prayers of the church for him, they will work for us. The church was praying the will of God for Peter's life. The angels of God go to work for us when we

pray the Word of God, which is the will of God. That
brings me to the next principle.

The Word of God Is the Will of God

I especially love the promise of God found in I John
5:14-15. It brings me such peace and comfort in prayer:
"This is the confidence we have in approaching God: that if
we ask anything according to his will, he hears us. And if
we know that he hears us – whatever we ask – we know
that we have what we have asked of him" (NIV). Before I
knew this principle, the scripture in Matthew 7:21 always
troubled my husband and me causing us constant concern.
The will of God was one of the main priorities in our lives:
"Not everyone who says to me, 'Lord, Lord,' will enter the
Kingdom of heaven, but only the one who does the will of
my Father who is in heaven" (Matthew 7:21, NIV). With
that said, it is obvious that praying the Lord's Prayer with
the statement, "Thy kingdom come, thy will be done in my
life as it is in heaven" was music to our ears. We wanted the
will of God in our lives. However, the question for me was
always: how do I know what the will of God is for my life?
How can I be assured I am in the will of God?

God is so gracious to alleviate our fears and meet us
where we are. He knew my struggle, my anxious thoughts,
and my true heart's desire to be in His perfect will. Let me
share with you how He lovingly, yet so simply conveyed
this truth to me. Here is the setting that brought this
wonderful revelation and peace to me instead of fear.

As I mentioned before, we moved to Rockwall, Texas upon a word from God my husband heard in his spirit during the Pastors' conference. Upon our arrival, we basked in the worship, weeping before God for weeks as He purified our hearts from hurt, rejection, and the pain of leaving the past behind to step into our future. The anointed teaching and preaching were like the oil of the Holy Spirit pouring over us at every service. We were being prepared for the days ahead beyond what we could think or imagine. We entered a sabbatical year of prayer and uncommon fellowship with the Holy Spirit — such special days — unlike any we have had since. It was time set apart from ministry. It was time alone with God.

We knew no one personally upon our arrival in Texas. We were there in obedience to the call of God to learn. We learned from the Pastors and Elders of the church as they taught. We learned from the voice of the Holy Spirit as He took what they said and fashioned it specifically to our lives and what He intended to do with us. We were there among thousands. Yet, we were alone with Him. We were on our special journey with the Holy Spirit much like Noah was in the ark safe and sound, while the rainstorm flooded the earth. We were lifted above the "busyness" of life alone with God until He opened the door and said it was time to come out. During this time, we gradually formed friendships that have lasted a lifetime.

Just a few months after our arrival and still within this sabbatical period I just described, the church held a two-day women's school covering all areas of a young mother's life: parenting, fashion, cooking, finances, etc. Most of those who attended had school-age or preteen children. The classes were taught by some of the Pastors' and Elders' wives. The Elder's wife who was scheduled to teach us how to balance our checkbooks that first day said something life-changing. She stopped before she even began the class and said, "I want to share three scriptures I pray for my husband daily with you. I want to be in agreement with him. Whatever scripture God has given to him, I write it down and pray it with him...because you know – 'The word of God is the will of God.'" She had no idea what she said meant to me! That phrase was exactly what I needed to hear. I felt like a light exploded within me. Of course, the Word of God is the will of God! Why didn't I ever see that before?

I was so relieved and thrilled at the same time! I had the answer! I knew the will of God now! Whatever I found in the Word of God was the will of God. From that day forward, I immediately began to weave the Word of God into my daily prayers within the outline of the Lord's Prayer. I soon discovered the next principle.

Notes:

1. Murdock, Mike *101 Wisdom Keys* p 28.

2. Willhite, B. J. and Doyle, Judy *How Much Faith Does It Take to Move the Hand of God* p 14.

Chapter Four
A Specific Word for Specific Problems

Inspired by the revelation that the Word of God is the will of God, I first searched the scriptures to confirm the pattern the Elder's wife had shown us that day. I saw that Jesus never argued with the Enemy during His temptation in the desert (Matthew Chapter 4). Instead, for each temptation, Jesus replied with the Word of God:

"Jesus answered, 'It is written, Man does not live by bread alone but by every word that comes from the mouth of God'" (Matthew 4:4, NIV; emphasis mine).

"Jesus answered him, 'It is also written, 'Do not put the Lord your God to test'" (Matthew 4:7, NIV; emphasis mine).

"Jesus said to him, 'Away from me Satan! For it is written: 'Worship the Lord your God and serve him only'" (Matthew 4:10, NIV; emphasis mine).

In the book of Revelation, as recorded by the apostle John, Jesus uses this same strategy against Satan when He returns to earth:

"Out of his mouth came a sharp double-edged sword" (Revelation 1:16, NIV).

"I will soon come to you and will fight against them with the sword of my mouth" (Revelation 2:16, NIV).

"Out of his mouth comes a sharp sword with which to strike down the nations" (Revelation 19:15, NIV).

In Ephesians Chapter 6, I noticed that Paul also admonishes us to put on the armor of God referring to the *"sword of the Spirit, which is the Word of God"* (verse 17). The Word of God is the only offensive part of the armor of God. It is intended to inflict injury to the Enemy. I discovered several powerful verses confirming the effectiveness of praying the Word of God. Having read them, I knew Satan was no match for the Word of God. The Word of God is stronger:

"So it is my word that goes out from my mouth: It will not return to me empty, but will accomplish what I desire and achieve the purpose for which I sent it" (Isaiah 55:11, NIV).

"Your word, O Lord, is eternal, it stands firm in the heavens" (Psalm 119:89, NIV).

"He sends his commands to the earth; his word runs swiftly" (Psalm 147:15, NIV).

"They overcame him by the blood of the Lamb and by the word of their testimony" (Revelation 12:11, NIV).

How to Pray Specific Prayers

In this section, I will give you some examples of how to apply specific Words to specific problems in your life. This has worked amazingly for my family and me. My husband and children have been the main focus of my prayers for many years. I learned "to pray before I say" anything in dealing with my husband or those in authority. I knew from experience, my efforts to correct problems in my husband's life usually fell on deaf ears. Even if he heard and agreed with me, there appeared to be no follow-through or enabling ability (grace) to do anything about the problem. At times, my "insights" would cause friction and walls of frustration to come between us. No one likes criticism, even if it is meant to be constructive. We all prefer encouragement.

Thankfully, I found a wonderful scripture that helped me in these situations. It opened my eyes and showed me I should go to my husband's spiritual authority – Jesus. Moreover, I was encouraged to trust the Lord to change or correct my husband. I learned to pray Proverbs 2:1 *"The king's heart is in the hand of the Lord; he directs it like a watercourse wherever he pleases* (NIV)." Next, I prayed the scripture that addressed the need in his life. If the need concerned our children, I prayed Malachi 4:6

"Turn the hearts of the fathers to their children (Father, turn John's heart to our children) *and the hearts of the children to their fathers"* (and let the hearts of our children be drawn to John) (NIV).

When He became frustrated at work, I prayed Proverbs 21:1 and followed it up with Psalm 90:12: *"Teach us (him) to number our (his) days aright, that we (he) may gain a heart of wisdom* (NIV)." I also used Exodus 17:12, *"Aaron and Hur held his (Moses) hands up – one on one side, one on the other – so that his hands remained steady till sunset* (NIV)." I would pray this scripture as follows: "Father, send John an Aaron and a Hur to hold his hands steady and stand beside him as he labors for You." If it was a financial matter, I prayed Matthew 25:21, *"Thou has been faithful over a few things, I will make thee ruler over many things* (KJV)." As I prayed these scriptures over him, within two or three days, his attitude would change toward the very thing I prayed about. For example:

- One evening he burst through the door and said, "We have got to spend more time with the girls! I have been a bear lately! Let's go on a bike ride tonight."

- Another night John came home and said, "We have got to take care of that insurance. I can't think about anything else. It has been on my mind all day!" Why had he been thinking about it all day? God was "directing his heart like a watercourse" (Proverbs 21:1, NIV).

- I noticed he started making a list in the morning during devotions. I didn't say anything but a few days later he mentioned, "You know, God has been telling me what to do in the morning, and I am getting so much done at the office now." I had tried for years to get him to make a daily "to-do list" as I did. He wouldn't listen to me, preferring to just deal with things as needed. However, he gladly listened to the instructions of the Holy Spirit and found a great sense of accomplishment as he dealt with things that were important from God's perspective.

I prayed the Word of God according to the will of God, and He heard my prayer. The beautiful thing about all of it is John thought it was his idea! These days, we laugh about it together, but he appreciates the fact I still pray for him and only give him advice when he asks for it.

This method is not limited to family, but it is also very effective when praying for leaders we served through the years, as well as the presidents of our nations. I may never have the opportunity to meet with the president or

CEO of a company where I am employed. However, I can have an audience with the One who can "direct their hearts like a watercourse" (Proverbs 21:1). I can pray the will of God for the president or leader. Many, many times I have prayed and seen results with these scriptures: *"Remove the wicked from the king's presence, and his throne will be established through righteousness"* (Proverbs 25:5b, NIV).

"Then the righteous will gather round (him) because of your good to (him)" (Psalm 142:7, NIV).

John 15:7 is true, *"If you remain in me and my words remain in you, ask whatever you wish, and it will be given you (NIV)."* I normally prefer the NIV version of most scriptures; however, for some reason, I especially like the word "abide" in the King James Version of this scripture, *"If you abide in me and my words abide in you, ye shall ask what you wish and it will be done unto you (John 15:7)."*

Specific Prayers for Your Children

The strategy for my children was a little different since they are under my authority. I learned to pray the Word of God over their challenges at school and with their friendships. The Lord gave me the following scripture: *"The entrance of the word gives light; it gives understanding to the simple"* (Psalm 119:130, NIV). I knew exactly what to do. I began to teach the girls the Lord's Prayer on the way to school in the morning with multiple scriptures woven in it. I knew the more of the Word I could get into their spirits, the more understanding they would have with their studies. It worked. The Word of God is stronger! Below is an example of that prayer based on the Lord's Prayer in Matthew 6:9-13 as taught by Dr. Larry Lea in his book, *Could You Not Tarry One Hour?*

THE LORD'S PRAYER

OUR FATHER WHICH ART IN HEAVEN, HALLOWED BE THY NAME

"I will praise thee; for I am fearfully and wonderfully made" (Psalm 139:14a, KJV).

Thank you for the blood of Jesus and for being:

1. Jehovah-Tsidkenu, my righteousness

   The righteous are bold as a lion, the wicked man flees with no one pursuing him (Proverbs 28:1, NIV).

2. Jehovah-M'Kaddesh, my sanctification

   "Create in me a clean heart, O God; and renew a right spirit within me" (Psalm 51:10, NIV).

3. Jehovah-Shalom, my peace

   I will trust in the Lord with all mine heart; and lean not unto mine own understanding. In all my ways acknowledge Him, and He shall direct my paths (Proverbs 3:6, KJV).

I choose to seek first the kingdom of God, and his righteousness, and all these things shall be added unto me (Matthew 6:33, KJV).

For all things work together for good to them that love God, to them who are the called according to His purpose (Romans 8:28, NIV).

4. Jehovah-Shammah, ever present with me

    You said to, "Call to me and I will answer you and tell you great and unsearchable things you do not know" (Jeremiah 33:3, NIV).

5. Jehovah-Rophe my healer

    "By his stripes we are healed" (Isaiah53:5d, NIV).

6. Jehovah-Jireh my provider

    "According to His riches in glory" (Philippians 4:19, NIV)

7. Jehovah-Nissi, our protector

    His banner over us is love (Song of Solomon 2:4b, NIV).

    His hedge of protection is around us (Job 1:10, NIV); *and*

    His favor guards us as a shield (Psalm 5:12b, NIV)

8. Jehovah-Rohi, the kind and gentle Shepherd

    He leads us beside the still waters and makes us lie down in green pastures (Psalm 23:2, KJV).

THY KINGDOM COME; THY WILL BE DONE IN MY LIFE AS IT IS IN HEAVEN:

- *Open my ears to hear what the Spirit is saying* (Proverbs 23:12, NIV).

- *Open my eyes to see in wisdom and revelation* (Ephesians 1:17, NIV).

- *Set a guard over my mouth and keep watch over the door of my lips* (Psalm 141:3, NIV).

- *May the words of my mouth and the meditation of my heart be pleasing in your sight, O Lord, my Rock and my Redeemer* (Psalm 19:14, NIV).

- *A soft answer turns away wrath, but a harsh word stirs up anger* (Proverbs 15:1, NIV).

- *Train my hands for war and my fingers for battle* (Psalm 144:1, NIV).

- *Whatever my hands find to do, help me to do it with all my might* (Ecclesiastes 9:10, NIV).

- *Direct my steps according to your Word* (Proverbs 16:9, NIV).

- *Teach me to number my days aright that I may gain a heart of wisdom* (Psalm 90:12, NIV).

FILL US WITH THE FRUIT OF THE SPIRIT:

* *Love, joy, peace, patience, kindness, goodness, faithfulness, gentleness and self-control* (Galatians 5:22, NIV).

In the name of Jesus and in the power of His blood, we bind the hindering spirits of frustration, confusion, and distraction off our lives, and we loose the Spirit of the Lord:

* *The Spirit of wisdom and understanding, knowledge and discernment and discipline* (Isaiah 11:2, Proverbs 14:16, Proverbs 6:23, NIV).

In the name of Jesus and in the power of His blood, we bind the hindering spirits of selfishness, jealousy, envy, fighting, and anger; we loose the spirit of love:

* *For love is patient, love is kind. It does not envy, it does not boast, it is not proud or rude or self-seeking, it is not easily angered or keep any record of wrongs. It does not delight in evil but rejoices in the truth. It always protects, always trusts, always hopes, always perseveres* (I Corinthians 13:4-7, NIV).

* *May the favor of the Lord our God rest upon us and may He establish the work of our hands for us* (Psalm 90:17, NIV).

And for mom and dad, our pastor, pastor bob, our teachers, ms. Paula and ms. Rachel, and our president of the united states.

- *"Remove the wicked from the king's presence, and his throne will be established in righteousness"* (Proverbs 25:5, NIV).

- *"Then the righteous will gather around him because of your goodness to him"* (Psalm 142:7, NIV).

- *Fulfill your purpose in him, O Lord, for your love endures forever – do not abandon the work of your hands* (Psalm 138:8, NIV).

GIVE US THIS DAY OUR DAILY BREAD:

We stand in agreement together for all our needs to be met:

a. _____

b. _____

c. _____

FORGIVE US OUR DEBTS AS WE FORGIVE OUR DEBTORS:

We choose to walk in love and forgiveness. Forgive me, Father, when I have offended you:

_____ (name specific offense).

AND LEAD US NOT INTO TEMPTATION BUT DELIVER US FROM EVIL:

- *"Put on the whole armor of God, that ye may be able to stand against the wiles of the devil"* (Ephesians 6:11, KJV).

- *We gird our loins about with truth; we put on the breastplate of righteousness. We shod our feet with the readiness of the gospel of peace and pull down the helmet of salvation. We take out our sword of the spirit and shield of faith.* (Ephesians 6:14-17, KJV).

THE HEDGE OF PROTECTION IS AROUND US:

- *"The angel of the Lord encamps around those that fear Him, and He delivers them"* (Psalm 34:7, NIV).

FOR THINE IS THE KINGDOM AND THE POWER AND THE GLORY FOREVER AMEN!

I also learned the power of the Word of God when it came to dealing with the challenging children my kids encountered at school. When my daughter was in elementary school, she came home discouraged and sad during the first week of school. Upon questioning her, I learned that none of her friends were playing with her or including her in their after school plans. Interestingly, at the time, the Pastor was teaching how to deal with people who oppose us. He emphasized it is not the person who is troubling us but a spirit manipulating him or her like a puppet on strings. I took that to heart and prayer. I used the scripture found in Psalm 101:8 to take authority over the spirits oppressing my little girl: "*Every morning I will put to silence all the wicked in the land; I will cut off every evildoer from the city of the Lord*" (NIV). I used this scripture in the name of Jesus and commanded the spirits to leave.

Now, remember, I was a very young mother at that point just learning to pray like this. I did not really know if it would work or not. I was praying much like the church praying for Peter's release. They did not have a lot of faith, but they had "enough faith to pray and move the hand of God."[1] They were surprised when Peter was released from prison and showed up at their prayer meeting. In the same way, I had enough faith to pray for my little girl. To my delight, at the end of the week, she came running to the car happy and smiling ear to ear. "Mom," she said, "All my friends played with me and invited me to a birthday party Friday night."

When we change things in the spirit realm, it manifests in the natural realm. "All truth is parallel."[2] I was taking "baby steps" but little by little, I learned the power of prayer, the power of the Word of God, and the authority we have in the Spirit to establish the kingdom of God on the earth.

I learned to overcome rejection in my children's lives with Luke 2:52, *"Jesus grew in wisdom and stature and in favor with God and men"* (NIV). Let it be so with my children. I prayed the promises of Deuteronomy Chapter 28 that they would be *the head and not the tail, above and not beneath.* When the Enemy attacked them, he would *stumble and fall.* When the Enemy came at them in one direction, *he would flee in seven.*

To overcome fearfulness, I prayed that they would be *"bold as a lion"* (Proverbs 28:1) and *"You have not given us a spirit of fear, but of power, and of love, and of a sound mind"* (II Timothy 1:7, KJV). The NIV uses the word "self-discipline" in place of "sound mind."

Before we move to the next chapter, I will share with you the life-changing scriptures that started my journey of praying the Word of God in every area of our lives. The Elder's wife shared these three scriptures with us on that momentous day to pray over our husbands:

"Blessed is the man (my husband, John), who does not walk in the way of the wicked, or stand in the way of sinners, or sit in the seat of mockers. But his delight is in the law of the Lord and in his law, he meditates day and night. He is like a tree by streams of water, which yields its fruit in season, whose leaf does not wither. Whatever he does shall prosper" (Psalm 1:1-3, NIV).

"The Spirit of the Lord will rest upon (my husband, John), the Spirit of wisdom and understanding, the Spirit counsel and power, the Spirit of knowledge and the fear of the Lord – and he will delight in the fear of the Lord" (Isaiah 11:2, 3, NIV),

"May the favor of the Lord rest upon (John); establish the work of his hands for hand, -yes, establish the work of his hands" (Psalm 90:17, NIV),

I learned in the following months and years that no matter what we faced, the Word of God is stronger! This brings us to our next level.

NOTES:

1. Willhite, B. J. and Doyle, Judy *How Much Faith Does It Take to Move the Hand of God* p 14.

2. Cerullo, Morris Proof Producers: *"What We Must Do to Work the Works of God"* p 335.

Chapter Five
Faith to Fight Within

Something very interesting developed within me the more I prayed the Word of God. As I prayed the Word of God daily, it was easy to commit it to memory. The more I memorized the Word of God, the more I applied it to my life. The more I prayed, memorized, and applied the Word, the more I thought about the Word. The more I implemented it into my life, the stronger and bolder I became. Soon, I realized I was not depressed anymore. When a challenge came my way, I drew my sword (Word of God) and took care of it. It was thrilling. All of this was taking place quietly in the place of prayer. No one knew what was happening in, for or through me except my husband.

I first recognized the fear was gone in a very unusual set of circumstances, which I will share at this point. A couple of intercessors from Chicago who visited our church's early morning prayer meetings in Rockwall invited my husband to come to Chicago to hold a prayer conference. The TBN network televised the Friday morning prayer meetings at the time. The representatives from the Chicago church were inspired to visit the prayer meetings due to the telecasts.

This was an exciting invitation for my husband, and he happily agreed. John's outgoing temperament is always ready for a challenge and this was just another wonderful adventure for him. Then they turned to me and said, "We want you to come with him." I was shocked. "Oh, no," I said. "You don't want me. I don't sing or do anything. Really, I don't do a-n-y-t-h-i-n-g" (I repeated slowly for emphasis). That did not deter them. They insisted I come with him with no expectations from me. Surprised and somewhat puzzled, we agreed and flew to Chicago within a couple of months.

We were picked up in a limousine and taken to the hotel where presidents usually stay in Chicago. We were somewhat shocked by such treatment and wondered why. John preached a powerful message that night inspiring everyone to pray. We were to be back at the church the next morning at 6:00 a.m. to lead the prayer meeting, which meant we had to get up at 4:00 a.m. to leave the hotel by 5:00 a.m. It was nearly midnight when we reached our hotel that evening.

Upon our arrival in the hotel room, John turned to me and said, "I had such a busy week I didn't have time to prepare anything for this conference. I guess I'll just stay up all night and prepare the messages for tomorrow." I could not believe it! There were four services the next morning, including the first-hour prayer session. I wanted to run back home. I was so mad at him and embarrassed! It was after midnight by this time and there was no way he could possibly be ready for the next day in just four short hours.

As he sat there, not at all upset, trying to figure out his strategy for the morning sessions, I spoke up and said, "Well, if you want me to, I could take a session and tell them how to pray for their loved ones." I could not believe the words were even coming out of my mouth! I had always been happy just to sit in the back of the room and never say a word to anyone and happy if no one said anything to me. John looked relieved and quickly agreed that would work. Looking back now, I can see that he instantly knew the messages to bring for the morning services *after* we decided to minister together as a team.

The next morning, the conference went as "smooth as clockwork." The 6:00 a.m. prayer meeting was strong and powerful. John gave his testimony in the next session, which inspired everyone to never give up. In the third session, I was sure the place would explode from the exuberant response. The last session was mine. Although I had never taught before in my life, this didn't seem to bother my husband at all as he introduced me to the church. (In the past, all I did was play the piano and even then, I could turn it in a way where I felt hidden from scrutiny). Surprisingly, though, when I stood to face over 2000 faces that morning, I felt absolutely no fear or hesitation at all.

All I could think about was, "I have the answer." The Word of God is the will of God. Pray the Word and all of heaven will go to work! It was the first step through a door God supernaturally opened and literally pushed me through. From that point forward, we traveled the nation and nations teaching prayer together and setting people free. If God can do this for me, He can do this for anyone no matter how shy, fearful, downcast or discouraged the person is. The Word of God is stronger!

Let me share the second vision I had as I prayed the Word of God. I knew I had become the warrior in the spirit realm I saw when I first began my journey of prayer. At this point, I saw myself lifting weights like a weight lifter – up and down, up and down, high over my head when I prayed specific scriptures for specific problems. I knew what it meant. The more I prayed the Word, the stronger I became. Praying the Word, confessing the Word, and implementing the Word build faith. *"Faith comes by hearing, and hearing by the word of God"* (Romans 10:17, KJV).

Something supernatural took place when my spirit heard my voice declaring the Word of God morning by morning – faith came!

"Do not let this Book of the Law depart from your mouth; meditate on it day and night, so that you may be careful to do everything written in it. Then you will be prosperous successful" (Joshua 1:8, NIV). The faith actions of keeping the Word of God in my mouth, meditating on it and walking in obedience to the Word of God, transformed me from within.

"The tongue has the power of life and death" (Proverbs 18:21, NIV). My tongue had life in it morning by morning. I continually prayed the scripture in conjunction with this one: *"Set a guard over my mouth and keep watch over the door of my lips"* (Psalm 141:3, NIV). I learned not only to pray the Word but also to only speak the Word of God. I learned I could "undo" my time in prayer in the heavens if my words did not line up with God's words that I had spoken in prayer that morning. I realized demons are "voice-activated." They prey on our negative words to gain access, strength, and power in our lives. They are fallen angels bent on harming us (I Peter 5:8) instead of serving us as the angels do (Hebrews 1:14).

"Again, truly I tell you that if two of you on earth agree about anything they ask for, it will be done for them by my

Father in heaven" (Matthew 18:19, NIV). When we pray the Word, God works for us. When we agree in prayer together, the power of the Spirit multiplies exponentially and, *"It will be done for them by my Father"* is a tremendous promise.

"If you, then, though you are evil know how to give good gifts to your children, how much more will your Father in heaven give good gifts to those who ask him?" (Matthew 7:11, NIV). I asked. I received. Answered prayer builds faith.

"The wicked man flees though no one pursues, but the righteous are bold as a lion" (Proverbs 28:1, NIV). The boldness I prayed for my husband day after day became a part of me. The seed of the Word I was declaring morning by morning took root in my heart and grew strong within (unknowingly to me).

Before we move on, let us look at a very inspirational story found in the book of Nehemiah. In adversity and discouragement, these people had the faith to fight. Their attitude and fortitude inspired me to fight for my family as well. In Nehemiah Chapter 4, the enemies of Israel rose up in opposition against the rebuilding of the wall around Jerusalem.

Nehemiah had been commissioned by King Artaxerxes to return to Jerusalem to rebuild the wall and repair the gates. However, three of the local residents,

Sanballat the Horonite, Tobiah the Ammonite official, and Geshem the Arab were upset that someone had come to promote the welfare of the Israelites (Nehemiah 2:10, NIV). They vehemently opposed the project. But despite the murmuring, complaining, and ridicule, Nehemiah continued the work. *"So we rebuilt the wall till all of it reached half its height, for the people worked with all their heart"* (Nehemiah 4:6, NIV). When the opposition saw the work continuing, they plotted to fight against Jerusalem to stop the progress. The threats, hard work, and even some of their Jewish neighbors discouraged the workers. In Nehemiah 4:10 we find, *"The strength of the laborers is giving out, and there is so much rubble that we cannot rebuild the wall"* (NIV).

This was no easy task. However, for this assignment, God had provided the leadership, resources, and the vision for restoration. Initially, the people gladly worked with all their hearts. But after a while, they lost focus and listened to the wrong voices. As long as they listened to the voice of God through Nehemiah, they had strength. When they listened to the voices of discouragement and negativity from their enemies, they lost heart.

Psalm 127:1-2 aptly fits this situation and our lives as well: *"Unless the Lord builds the house, its builders labor in vain. Unless the Lord watches over the city, the watchmen stand guard in vain"* (NIV). As long as the builders were inspired by the promise of God, they had strength and energy. Once their eyes looked at their challenging storms instead of directing their focus above the storm to the end result, their strength gave out. In our own lives, unless we depend on the power of the Spirit of God within, our natural strength will wane and give out. *"'Not by might, not by power, but by my Spirit,' says the Lord Almighty"* (Zechariah 4:6, NIV).

The people could only build the wall to half its height when they worked in their strength. Likewise, we cannot build according to God's plan until we learn to combine the supernatural strength of the Spirit with our natural abilities. Our natural strength is no match for the insidious attacks the Enemy plans for our lives. He plots. He plans. He strategizes and causes people to come into our lives who will harm us. He devises schemes to deceive.

Nehemiah was not discouraged. He had a word from God to rebuild the wall and he intended to fulfill his mission. He recognized they needed the power of God with them. After Nehemiah posted families at the lowest part of the walls with weapons of swords, spears, and bows, he declared, *"Don't be afraid of them. Remember the Lord who is great and awesome and fight for your brothers, your sons and your daughters, your wives and your houses"* (Nehemiah 4:14, NIV). He armed the people for war. Half of the men stood guard, while the other half worked. Those who worked strapped their swords to their sides.

Due to the extensive area, the instruction was clear, *"Wherever you hear the sound of the trumpet, join us there. Our God will fight for us!"* (Nehemiah 4:20, NIV). The work continued day and night until the wall was completed!

In the same way, I learned to live with the sword of Spirit daily at my side. I recognized the Enemy never rests. I determined I would not stand idly by and watch the assaults on my husband, children, friends, and relatives. I learned to use the Word of God in prayer to combat every attack. If we do not pray, who will? If we don't learn to fight with the sword of the Spirit against the wiles of the Enemy, who will? *"Unless the Lord builds the house, the builders labor in vain"* (Psalm 127:1, NIV). I do not want to try to build my house, family or ministry in my own strength. That would be an exercise in futility because we can only overcome and drive the Enemy out of our lives with the Spirit of God. Even then, the Enemy will return but the Word of God is stronger!

Chapter Six
See Through the Storm

Now we have learned the principles of prayer that develop the strength and power within, it is time to address our approach to the storms of life. Just as most storm clouds block the sunshine and cause darkness, one of the first things we experience when the storms of life blow is the loss of clarity. Suddenly, all we can see is the problem as it looms before us.

In difficult times, we must learn to see through the storm, lift our eyes above it, and look to our heavenly Father for help. It does not matter what we are facing or the circumstances around us. The Word of God is true; hence, we must fill our eyes with the Word to see through the storm. *"When the storm has swept by, the wicked are gone but the righteous stand firm forever"* (Proverbs 10:25, NIV). The righteous stand firm because *"The word of God stands firm in the heavens"* (Psalm 119:89, NIV). This storm did not take God by surprise. He is not shaken. His Word is not shaken. His promises are still true. He still has a wonderful *"hope and future"* (Jeremiah 29:11, NIV) planned for us. We must lift our eyes and focus on the Word of God, which is stronger. Following is an encouraging word that helps us "see" through life's storms.

Intercession Brings Revelation

Through revelation, we can know what to do in every situation. We can understand what to do with our children, husbands and in whatever crisis or challenge the storm brings. *"If you hold to my teaching and you are really my disciples, then you will know the truth and the truth will set you free"* (John 8:31, NIV).

Our church needed to expand the sanctuary, which meant removing a wall so there could be a larger capacity. For nine months, the county refused to give us the permit citing parking as the problem. This was erroneous since the other businesses in the shopping center were not open on Sundays and there was no shortage of parking. We knew this was a spiritual battle. It is very difficult for any church in San Diego to get the proper zoning for expansion or building. Another Pastor in San Diego spent $300,000 in fees and permits but never received permission to build on his property. In the same way, we were in a storm and could see no solution.

During one of our early morning prayer times, as we were walking and praying in the sanctuary with our blueprints on the floor, our eyes were suddenly opened. We saw the answer. We saw through the storm of confusion and resistance. The stage area designated for the sanctuary was not on the blueprint. Once the stage was shown to the county, the seating capacity for the church services was less.

The day this new information was presented, the supervisor, instead of the regular clerk happened to be in the office on duty. After he looked over the presentation, he saw no problems and granted permission. The clerk who had been rejecting all our documentation for nine months returned from lunch just as the supervisor was concluding his inspection. She actually screamed at him as he signed the permit, "No! No! No! There's not enough parking! Another building is zoned for that parking lot!" His reply was very firm as he signed the approval, "That building has not been built and may never be built. They have plenty of parking." God intervened for us. Not only did He show us the solution, but He also directed us to the right person at the right time.

It is the Devil's business to blind our eyes and to stop our ears. He does this so we will not know the truth. He wants to discourage us. He wants us to listen to his deceiving voices so we remain bound in darkness, not knowing which way to go or what to do.

Though seeing, they do not see. Though hearing they do not understand. In them is fulfilled the prophecy of Isaiah. You will be ever hearing but never understanding, ever seeing but never perceiving for this people's heart had become calloused. They hardly hear with their ears and they have closed their eyes. Otherwise, they might see with their eyes, hear with their ears and understand with their hearts, turn and I would heal them. <u>*But blessed are your eyes because you see and your ears because you hear.*</u> (Matthew 13:16, NIV; emphasis mine)

"I am the light of the world. <u>*Whoever follows me will never walk in darkness but will have the Light of life*</u>*"* (John 8:12, NIV; emphasis mine). We see from these scriptures that God can and will open our eyes to look beyond the problems and see the solution – to see through the storms.

Before we move on to the next level, let's consider a biblical example. Romans Chapter 4 shows us the faith of the patriarch, Abraham. He was 99 years old and had held onto a promise for 25 years! Romans Chapter 4 declares that Abraham *"faced the fact that his body was as good as dead."* However, Abraham was fully *"persuaded that God had power to do what He had promised"* and *"He did not waver through unbelief regarding the promise of God."* But *"Against all hope, Abraham, in hope believed... and because of that, he became the father of many nations."* Abraham realized that facts are only temporary! They change! But the truth of our

God is eternal! It *"stands firm in the heavens"* (Psalm 119:89, NIV) and never changes.

Abraham learned to see through the storm of barrenness, disappointment, and perhaps disillusionment. He waited twenty-five years for the promise of God to be fulfilled. Only after the Lord paid him a personal visit did Abraham finally see through this storm. God changed his name from Abram (exalted father) to Abraham (father of many nations) to get Abraham's words in line with the promise. Hearing his new name day after day came in line with God's promise, *"Your off spring will be a numerous as the stars"* (Genesis 15:5, NIV).

Abraham saw through his storm every time he looked up at the stars in heaven. No longer did he hear Abram (exalted father) daily and only see Ishmael, the son born of the Egyptian maid, Hagar. He heard Abraham (father of many nations) every day. At night, he saw the stars too numerous to count and remembered God's promise. His vision cleared, and he received His promise. Seeing and hearing bring us to the next level of strength.

Chapter Seven
Hear in the Storm

When the black storm clouds bring severe thunderstorms and the dangerous tornadoes blast our lives, the howling wind, crashing thunder and hard-driving rain makes it very difficult for us to hear or think clearly. Panic, fear, and terror are just a few emotions in all of us as we run to the storm cellar to escape the impending danger. Similarly, when storms of adversity hit us: lies, threats, and accusations it can be very difficult to get past the hurtful words hurled at us. Our minds reel and replay over and over the scenarios fueled by the worry we may or have encountered.

Natural storms and those from the Enemy are noisy. They are designed to block our hearing. They are ugly. They are meant to destroy, distract, and derail us from our path. The Enemy is a *"roaring lion seeking whom he may devour"* (I Peter 5:8, KJV). It does not matter who we are, where we are in our life's journey or what we are trying to do for God, he will attack us. The storms can hit our children, marriages, work or businesses, health, families or ministries. Like I mentioned earlier, "Storms in life are not an option; we must simply learn to fight."

I found the best thing to do in the middle of a storm is to silence the Enemy with Scripture. In Matthew 14:27, the first thing Jesus said to the disciples was, *"Take courage. It is I. Don't be afraid"* (NIV). I pray Psalm 101:8 every morning when my husband is struggling. *"Every morning I put to silence all the wicked in the land"* (NIV), I put to silence the wicked spirits and say, "You quit speaking to him. You quit causing doubt, confusion, and distraction in his life." This scripture and the authority of God's Word spoken over this situation stills the storm in his life.

When bad attitudes tried to rear their ugly heads in my children, I took authority over those spirits and I said, "You cannot speak to my children any longer. I take authority over you in Jesus' name. I silence you!" The spirits have to obey the Word of God. When you speak with the authority of God's Word, the brewing storm always dissipates.

When our home was disrupted or filled with disharmony or even now, if there are problems at the office, I take authority over that spirit and silence it by saying, "You can't speak." I take my stand and resist it. *"Resist the devil and he will flee from you"* (James 4:7, NIV), When thoughts that do not line up with the Word of God assault my mind, I resist them. I do not give place to them. I silence them with these scriptures, and they still the storm. Speaking the scriptures out loud stops the harassment in the mental realm. The mind cannot hear the noisy accusations of the storm when the mouth is speaking the words of God.

After we have silenced the Enemy and the noise level is down, it is time to hear what the Spirit of God is saying to us about the storm and to declare the Word. How do I get the Word? I simply ask, "Lord, what are You saying about this situation?" It may be very obvious. It may be a Word I have heard and used many times or it may be something new. The key is to hear the voice of the Holy Spirit to bring peace to the storm within. There is nothing like hearing the voice of the Spirit as He whispers the divine insights needed or to have a scripture leap off the page that is the Word for a specific storm.

If I do not hear anything specific at first, I simply pray, *"Thy kingdom come. Thy will be done"* until God sends a Word. Our world is noisy, so I take steps to quiet the noise around me. I turn off the television and radio, as well as put my phone on silent for a season. I get rid of all possible distractions and interruptions, so I can press into God. That means to get quiet in His presence and to listen for His voice. He will send a Word for every storm. Once

I hear the specific Word (scripture), I pray it into the middle of that storm. The storm weakens because the Word of God is stronger. I invite the God of this universe to get involved. All of heaven goes to work for me against the storm!

The loud turbulence within the storm is meant to distract you. The Enemy wants to drown out the voice of God in our lives. The loud, intimidating voices in this world keep our ears from being tuned in to the voice of God, the only voice that will bring the words of life for you and your family. Mark 4:24 is very clear about this matter: *"Consider carefully what you hear...with the measure you use, it will be measured to you and even more."*

Never forget how imperative it is to keep your ears tuned in to God. He is speaking to us every day. *"The Sovereign Lord has given me an instructed tongue, to know the word that sustains the weary. He wakens me morning by morning, wakens my ear to listen, like one being taught"* (Isaiah 50:4, NIV; emphasis mine). The Word of God is going forth for our children every morning. There is a Word from heaven for our family members every morning. There is a Word for the storms we face every morning! It is up to us to get our ears in tune, so we know what God wants us to speak into the storm.

Chapter Eight
Speak to the Storm

Let us look at Jesus as our example of speaking to storms. In John Chapter 6 and Matthew Chapter 8, we find the disciples in the middle of storms. Their reaction is not much different from most of us. They panicked and were afraid.

The disciples were in the middle of the will of God when the storm hit. It was God's will for them to go to the other side of the lake despite the storm. Jesus was even in the boat during one of these storms. When the billowing waves placed the boat in danger, the disciples ran to Jesus, woke Him up, and complained to Him, "Lord! Don't You even care? We are about to perish! Don't You know there is a storm raging?"

How many of us, when a storm rages in our lives, repeat the disciples' words, "Lord, don't you see this storm? Don't you care about us?" It is helpful to listen to the words Jesus spoke to His disciples in a storm, *"Don't be afraid."* (John 6:20, NIV). In another instance, He said to them, *"You of little faith. Why are you afraid?"* (Matthew 8:26, NIV). He then rebuked the storm and said, *"Quiet! Be still,"* (Mark 4:39, NIV) or *"Peace, be still,"* KJV). He spoke to the storm and it obeyed.

Did Jesus not give us the same power and authority He operated in when He departed this earth? *"All authority in heaven and on earth has been given to me. Therefore, go and make disciples of all nations, baptizing them in the name of the Father and of the Son and of the Holy Spirit, and teaching them to obey everything I have commanded you. And surely, I am with you always, the very end of the age"* (Matthew 28:18-30, NIV). Jesus expects us to follow His example, speak peace to our storms, our troubled souls, the storms of others, and to "fear not." He expects us to believe the storms will obey our authoritative command to *"Be still,"* just as the storm obeyed Jesus.

Many times when storms arise, we will be buffeted because we are doing the will of God. The Enemy wants us to think the storm has hit our lives because we have sinned, been disobedient or we are out of the will of God. Numerous accusations will assault our minds to distract us from the call of God upon our lives, to cause fear, turmoil, and exasperation. However, the words we speak in our storms are not just for the powers and principalities of darkness to hear. The words we speak will build our own faith, for *"Faith comes hearing and hearing from the Word"* (Romans 10:17, NIV). The Word we speak is heard by our own ears and drops into our Spirits building our faith. Each morning we speak, our ears hear our mouths and the words drop into our spirits.

Notice I said to pray the Word out loud. Thinking the Word of God is not as effective as praying it out loud. The demonic powers of darkness causing the storm cannot "hear" our thoughts. They cannot read our minds. They only know what we are thinking by the words of our mouths and actions. The spoken Word of God stills the storm and builds our faith. The angels pick up the spoken Word of God. The spoken Word of God drives out fear and ushers in the peace of God, the power of God, and the presence of God.

Chapter Nine
Walk Out of the Storm

As we have seen previously, some storms dissipate with the spoken Word, "Peace, be still." There are times, however, when a faith action is required. A faith action is exactly what it sounds like – an action taken in faith. It is an action prompted by the Holy Spirit in conjunction with prayer. A faith action is an action we take believing it is in obedience to the Spirit of God. In the book of James, Rahab is commended for her faith action of hiding the spies in Jericho. Her action saved her entire family. Abraham was also commended for his obedience to the Spirit when he offered his son of promise, Isaac, in faith believing God could raise him up to life again. Faith action is mentioned in James 2:17-18, *"In the same way, faith by itself, if it is not accompanied by action, is dead…I will show you my faith by what I do."*

Some storms require faith actions from us. We see an example of this in Peter's life. In Matthew 14:22-31, Jesus put the disciples in a boat and sent them to the other side by themselves, while He went into the hills to pray. Later that evening, He walked out to them on the water. The disciples cried out in fear when they saw a "ghost" headed in their direction, walking on the water. They were petrified.

Peter eventually managed to say, *"Lord, if it's you...tell me to come to you on the water."* The reply Peter heard required faith to arise in him. Jesus said, *"Come, come to Me."* Jesus was asking Peter to get out of the boat and walk into the storm.

Once we have silenced the voice of the Enemy, received God's Word for the storm, and spoken that Word into the storm, a faith action is usually necessary. During your prayer time, the Lord will give you something to do in the natural just as He did to Peter. It is not a bad thing when the Lord gives you an assignment. It actually stretches your faith somewhat and many times forces fear and apprehension to leave as the walk of obedience begins.

Some time ago, my husband and I struggled in a financial storm that lasted for several years. I prayed Deuteronomy Chapter 28 that we would be *"the head and not the tail...above and not beneath...blessed when we go out and blessed when we come in..."* The Lord told me to get our taxes in order. This was my first faith action assignment of many I would receive on this journey to financial freedom. I sent all of our documentation for the taxes to our CPA in

Texas. However, after several weeks then months with no response, we became very concerned. We could not get him to return our phone calls, faxes or emails. When a storm is raging, the Enemy tries to block our efforts in every way possible.

I decided to make this a special focus with specific Words (scriptures) for this storm. I got out my prayer notebook and began to write down what God told me about the situation and the scriptures to overcome. It is good to keep a prayer journal because the Lord will tell us how to pray and what to do. He will give us the strategy to win the battle.

As I prayed over this situation, the Lord said, "Kathy, your friend is offended with you." The scripture He gave me to pray was 2 Corinthians 10:5. It says we do not wage war the way the world does but that our weapons are *"mighty to the pulling down of strongholds"* (NIV). I spoke into the spirit realm and said, "I tear down the arguments and the pretensions that the Enemy has planted in this man's mind." And I prayed, "Lord, send Your Holy Spirit to him and begin to work in this situation."

I prayed specific scriptures all week long. On Friday, I knew it was time to send a fax and what to put in the fax. This was my faith action.

1) I prayed specific scriptures (the Word of God) over the problem

2) God gave me an assignment (faith action) to send a fax – notice it was not a phone call

3) He told me what to say in the fax

Now, this was not new. We had sent the CPA multiple faxes before with no response. However, it was different in the spirit realm now because we had prayed all week. It was time. The Lord had prepared the way. He said, "Kathy, send him a fax. Give him a brief update on your family. Tell him what has been going on in your life. Then, ask him if there's anything else he needs."

These were such simple instructions to follow yet so very effective. Now, remember, I had been praying all week over his mind, tearing down those strongholds, coming against them and asking the Holy Spirit to work in this situation. After I sent the fax, I walked to someone else's office to talk to the person when I heard my office phone ring. Who do you think was on the line? In his rich Texas accent, he said, "Kathy? You'll never guess who this is!" He said, "I was just sittin' here thinkin' about you!"

Now, why was he thinking about me? Because I had been praying specifically for him all week long! I talked to him for just a few minutes, and I said, "Robert, is there anything else you need?"

He said, "Kathy, you know, I'm going to get those taxes together for you today! You will have them the first of next week. I promise you that."

Again, I said, "Well, Robert, is there anything you need? Is there something I left out?"

He said, "Well, there were a couple of things, but I looked for them and I found them on the back page."

As I talked to him on the phone that day, I learned that his daughter had developed epilepsy. He had two deaths in his family, and he was the executor over the deceased's estates. He was under tremendous, personal pressure. The Enemy had blown several storms into his life!

His personal storms affected our lives and specifically our taxes. Nevertheless, he was true to his word. Those tax returns were on my desk the following Monday morning as promised! In addition to that, we got a much-needed tax refund that year. Our financial blessing in the form of the tax refund was held up or bound up in the spirit realm. The spirit realm was changed through prayer and our blessing was released.

The Enemy does not want us to come through this life blessed. He does not want us to succeed. He does not want us to become *"the head and not the tail… above and not beneath… the lender and not the borrower"* promised in Deuteronomy Chapter 28. Anything he can do to cause confusion, obstacles or delays, he will do.

I have found the Word of God is true. It does not return void but accomplishes what it has been sent to do (Isaiah 55:11). The Word of God is the will of God. He hears our prayers, and we receive what we ask of Him when the requests come in line with the will of God for our lives. The Word of God is the sword of the Spirit in the spirit realm. It tears down those things that are coming against us and builds a wall of protection and favor upon our lives.

I am so glad I learned to pick up the sword of the Spirit and apply it to my life. I encourage you to glean Words for the storms that come. Whatever is needed, the Holy Spirit wants to sit beside us and reveal the specific Word to us.

"Open my eyes that I may see wonderful things in your law" (Psalm 119:18, NIV).

"Speak out His words and let them frame a life full of blessing for you!" [1]

"Through faith we understand that the worlds were framed by the Word of God" (Hebrews 11:3, NIV).

Notes:

1. Copeland, Kenneth and Gloria From Faith to Faith: *A Daily Guide to Victory* page April 14.

Chapter Ten
Ride Out the Storm

There is a third type of storm we may face in life. It will be a major storm of hurricane or tsunami proportion. This storm is different. Hence, it will require a different strategy.

Paul experienced such a storm as he journeyed by ship to Rome. He had to ride out a storm of hurricane strength. It raged against their ship for weeks. All the cargo and tackle were thrown overboard in the midst of the storm to try to save the ship. Paul wrote that after many days of not seeing sun or stars, hope was lost (Acts Chapter 27).

Sometimes life's storms may last weeks, months or even years. What can we do? Stand firm in faith! There are times to speak to the storm, and it will dissipate. Other times, we must get out of the boat like Peter did and walk out of the storm by faith. Then there are times when we simply have to ride through the storm.

That was Paul's plight in Acts Chapter 27. He did not have any control over his circumstances as a prisoner in chains and at the mercy of decisions made by others for him. He had no choice. The soldiers surrounding him listened to the owner of the ship for counsel, instead of Paul's prophetic warning of bad weather and danger ahead. They were determined to press on to a better harbor for the winter on their journey to Rome. We may find ourselves in similar situations when we have no control of the ship (company, church, and ministry) and decisions are made despite repeated warnings from knowledgeable sources.

When we find ourselves in a storm of this magnitude, there may be no escape and we have to ride the ship down. Many may want to "jump ship." However, it is better to stay on a sinking ship in the will of God than to jump into the ocean of supposed safety out of the will of God. Notice Paul's admonition to the centurion and soldiers when the sailors let the lifeboat down to escape, *"Unless these men stay with the ship you cannot be saved. So the soldiers cut the ropes that held the lifeboat and let it fall away"* (Acts 27:31, 32, NIV). In their despair, they decided to listen to Paul, whereas before, they ignored his warning not to leave the port. Why did they decide to listen to Paul? They recognized he had strength from within that carried a message of hope. He had a word from God that none would be lost. The ship would be lost, but there would be no loss of life. They would all be saved.

The beautiful part of this story is the appearance of the angel to encourage him, *"Last night an angel of the God whose I am and whom I serve stood beside me and said, 'Do not be afraid, Paul. You must stand trial before Caesar; and God has graciously given you the lives of all who sail with you.' So keep up your courage, men, for I have faith in God that it will happen just as he told me"* (Acts 27:23-25). Notice one of the first things the angel said to him, *"Do not be afraid, Paul."* The Lord knows we struggle with this emotion and is always so careful to console and encourage us to take courage. It pleases Him when we embrace His words and drive fear out of our lives, *"For God did not give us a spirit of fear, but a spirit of power, of love and of a sound mind"* (II Timothy 2:7, KJV). Paul had no fear. He presented a picture of hope to the centurion and soldiers.

When we encounter storms of this magnitude, it may destroy our life's work. However, God's will for our lives will not be aborted. We will arrive safely on another shore. The Lord will send another ship along to carry us into the destiny He has designed for us. This scripture will prove true: *"And we know that in all things God works for the good of those who love him, who have been called according to His purpose"* (Romans 8:38, NIV).

I have always found great consolation in Joseph's words in Egypt: *"You intended to harm me, but God intended it for good to accomplish what is now being done, the saving of many lives"* (Genesis 50:20, NIV). In this passage, although

Joseph's brothers intended to harm him, God's intervention, purpose, and plan for his life prevailed for the saving of a nation. In his storm, Joseph lost his identity and his family. But he did not lose his dreams or the gifts within. He remained in his storm (prison) until the king sent for him. The gifts within were evident at every step of his journey until he finally reached the destination planned by God, *"for the saving of many lives."*

From these scriptures, we can take comfort that no matter what storm comes our way or how much destruction and harm the Enemy plans for us, God will turn it around for our good. Satan wanted Paul to perish. He tried to kill him at sea but when that failed, he sent a poisonous serpent to murder him. The power and purpose of God prevailed. Paul simply shook it off. He had an anointing within him to be released upon the island of Malta.

In Acts Chapter 28, no lives were lost, and the people on the island welcomed them with *"unusual kindness"* by helping them build a fire due to the rain and cold. The chief official of the island took them into his estate. Paul laid hands on his sick father and healed him, as well as the rest of the sick on the island were cured. These healings brought great favor and provision for their time on the island. The gifts of healing within Paul were used to forever change the people of this island. God caused *"things to work together for good"* (Romans 8:28, NIV). The original ship was lost, but Paul's destiny was Rome. He completed his journey on another ship.

We have encountered storms in our lives of these magnitudes. The helplessness can be overwhelming when the wrong decisions are made despite repeated warnings. During these changing scenes of life, the Holy Spirit is our comfort. Inevitably, when the storms seem to blow everything away, our ship always finds a port where people need the gifts that reside within us, much like Paul.

The first storm of this magnitude blew us into Rockwall, Texas, thirteen hundred miles from Virginia. We were leaving behind thirteen years of youth ministry in a major denomination and heading to a new charismatic land of power and glory. For several years, the new ministry ship carried us around the world and across our nation many times. We developed gifts within that forever changed us and brought hope and strength to many others. However, that ship crashed in a storm of media exposé. Repeated warnings from intercessors, prophets, and friends were ignored. Consequently, a national ministry that spearheaded a national prayer movement ended.

We swam to shore, and I found a safe harbor at a very stable church in North Dallas that had been established for well over fifty years. My life drastically changed. I moved from speaking to thousands to working as a part-time administrative assistant in the music department. It was a good yet difficult season in which I mourned the loss of a national vision, friends, financial provision, and ministry.

As I struggled through the storm, I began to see the people around me and their needs. I thought I was only going to be in the church music department temporarily and did not want to get involved. However, God is always at work. He pulled at my heartstrings on behalf of my co-workers. I finally relented and said, "Okay, Lord, I will pray for these people." My thoughts at that time were the same as the disciples in the sinking boat in the middle of the lake. "Lord, don't you care we perish in this storm?"

Our circumstances were dire financially. John worked out of state two to three weeks every month. I drove an hour to work after I dropped my youngest to school in the mornings, and my teenage daughter drove 30 minutes in the opposite direction to high school. I was trying to find balance with the girls' school schedules and activities, John's travel schedule, and then make some sense of our lives again! Despite my personal storm, the gifts within were still in operation. Despite the loss of the national ministry we had given our lives to for years, God still wanted to use the *gifts within us* for the people in the harbor of safety I was living in (working) eight hours a day.

Listen to this truth and you will see why God was tugging at my heart to help those around me. *"The best place to start receiving is by giving to others. By helping someone else, we grow in Christian maturity, we help ourselves in the process, and our needs are met as we provide for others."* [1]

As I began to pray for my new relationships at the office, the Lord gave me accompanying *faith actions* for each member of the office staff. Although it would be difficult to address the problems I saw in their lives, I remembered the teaching of Pastor Willhite in our morning prayer meetings: *"If we are not willing to be used by God to answer our prayers, we may be praying in vain."* [2]

This was not a small church by any means and some of the staff had served together for over 25 years. They had known and worked together for so long, there were many undercurrents between them. God gave me the assignment to pray for them. As I prayed, I received faith action assignments to complete. One by one, I went to the members of the office and talked to them. I encouraged them to forgive one another. It was amazing how the Spirit of God worked in their hearts. All of these co-workers were fifteen to twenty years my senior. I was the youngest on staff; yet, they listened to the voice of God within my voice. *"God speaks not only to us, but through us."*[3] We just have to be willing vessels. Two of the staff members had been close friends twenty years prior. They forgave one another and re-established their friendship. The others who were at odds with one another for several years due to unresolved issues agreed it was time to let it go. The undercurrents ceased.

Instead of listening to office accusations, I would walk out into the hall or go for a drink of water.

Little by little, change was brought to the office. I learned to love each one of them. I found a divine principle at work. You love the ones you pray for. The love of God began to flow through me to them. *"We know that we have passed from death to life, because we love each other...we ought to lay down our lives for our brothers and sisters...let us not love with words or speech but with actions and truth"* (I John 3:18, NIV). Ed Cole, who carried a tremendous anointing to inspire the men of our nation to fulfill their God-ordained roles in the home expressed this truth extremely well, *"You become intimate with the One to whom you pray, the one for whom you pray and the one with whom you pray."*[4]

This story really has a happy-ever-after ending. My husband and I encouraged a single mom working in the office as a file clerk to go back to school to get her teaching degree in music. She fell in love with one of her professors, married him, and the school where her children attended implemented a kindergarten music class just for her to teach! The Word of God is stronger.

Notes:

1. Collins, Gary E. *How to Be a People Helper* p 204.

2. Willhite, Bob *Why Pray?* p 34.

3. Ortberg, John *The Life You Have Always Wanted: Spiritual Disciplines for Ordinary People* p 153.

4. Cole, Edwin Louis *Maximized Manhood* p 79.

Chapter Eleven
New Beginnings

Just as Paul left Malta (the island of safety from the horrendous storm) and sailed to Rome, I left that church office a little over two years later on another ship toward our destiny. The destiny was California where we still live more than twenty years later. I did not want to take the ship to California. When I felt a move was imminent, I grieved for months in my spirit over the loss of my new friends and the state I love, Texas. It was a strategic move in the life of our family. I knew if we moved to California, there was a great probability our girls would marry and establish homes there. I did not want that to happen. I wanted to live in Texas, not so far away from my family in Arkansas: parents, grandparents, siblings, cousins, etc. However, this was not to be.

My husband and I relocated our family to California and eventually started a church. John received a revelatory message that helped me settle the storm of distress within. The title of the message was, "The Seed Does Not Have a Choice Where It Is Sown." I knew the message was for me. I was "to bloom where I was planted." I did not have a choice. We established a church and served as founding Pastors for fifteen years. In God's divine plan for our lives, His will for our family was California. Our girls did marry men from California. Both have established businesses and homes here and have blessed us with three beautiful grandchildren.

The storms did not cease although we crossed to the other side of the country. It was much like the disciples with Jesus in the boat when they crossed to the other side of the lake. A demon-possessed man in the country of Gadarenes awaited Jesus and the disciples after the storm. The good news is he was delivered! Upon establishing our church, several storms battered us. John developed horrible weekly migraines that usually lasted three days and only stopped after a visit to the emergency room. These left him exhausted and debilitated. It took months to find a cure after much prayer and persistence.

I worked as an administrative assistant with an international ministry to help fund the startup costs of the church. Again, my drive was an hour to and from work. Unexpectedly, our relatively new van started to have transmission problems. We had it replaced – seven times!

This storm lasted for months. In the midst of the breakdowns, I found myself walking in the rain, calling tow trucks and rental cars while struggling to get to and from work. However, we survived the storm. Finally, my husband, who is not a mechanic, crawled under the vehicle and discovered a bent pan that caused the transmission fluid to leak and ruin each of the transmissions. The van was fixed and served our church for many, many years. The storms initially targeted our health and finances, but we overcame.

The Enemy was relentless and other storms brew in the horizon. They would hit different areas of our lives. They targeted the leadership of the church. People blew in, and some blew out. We faced storms of divorce among staff members, strife among church members, as well as staff members, and pornographic addiction in leadership. Moreover, we faced literal firestorms that burned the surrounding communities and the loss of several families who relocated out of state. We faced economic storms when the economy fell and devastated many who became unemployed or suffered business failures. Storms engulfed our girls as they struggled to find the will of God for their lives in their relationships, education, and careers. These raging storms battered us on every side. They blew into our lives incessantly. But with each storm, we only grew stronger.

We also experienced great deliverance through the storms just like the man of Gadarenes. Our church grew from a few couples in our home to a new church launched in a beautiful community center. Marriages were healed, weddings took place, and babies were dedicated. Drug addicts were delivered. Hope returned to the downcast and hurting. We rejoiced for the many people who were saved, lives restored, bodies healed and business ventures that succeeded. We had many happy days. But we also had sad ones. We walked *"through the valley of the shadow of death"* with the elderly, and, unfortunately, with the young. All in all, it was a wonderful season of our lives that flourished in four locations – from our home to the community center, to a shopping center complex, and finally a church building.

We recognized though that seasons come and seasons go. The Lord seems to have new assignments for us every 13 to 15 years. Our last assignment embraced a new level of ministry that has always been on my husband's heart. As the "winds of change" began to blow again at our ship of ministry, a new venture emerged. This time, it encompassed an outreach to veterans from the church. As the call to John's spirit became louder and clearer, we realized a gentle storm was blowing him in a new direction. It was not a horrible life-threatening storm this time. It was more of a gentle wind tugging at his heart.

Four years ago, we re-directed the ship and launched into the hospice ministry as a full-time outreach from the church. John's heart is full, flourishing, and fulfilled as he walks with many as they enter eternity.

I found a safe harbor once again at the international ministry I mentioned earlier where I initially went to work to fund the church plant in California. I told them during the interview I would work for one year only. After the church launch, I would no longer be available. I reiterate, "Our plans are not always God's plans." His ways are definitely above our thoughts. *"For my thoughts are not your thoughts, neither are you ways my ways,' declares the Lord"* (Isaiah 55:8, NIV).

A year-and-half later when I turned in my resignation, I was offered a part-time position. This was definitely beneficial for our family, less financial burden for the church, and a great outlet for the national and international call upon our lives. I worked part-time for the fifteen years we served as Pastors in the church and now, I have been with this ministry for twenty years. It is hard to believe. One year stretched to twenty. In this harbor of safety, the same thing has happened as it did in Dallas, Texas. I formed friendships and connected spiritually with the staff. The gifts within emerged again to find expression in chapel services and prayer meetings, which were at one point transmitted to our offices around the world in Canada, London, France, and Kenya.

Weekly prayer meetings with staff members are a joy and teaching prayer is my passion. Dr. Morris Cerullo and his wife, Theresa, are precious missionary evangelists who have established the kingdom of God around the world for over 75 years. I do believe he is a modern-day apostle Paul. It has been an honor to serve them and their vision for the world. This path of my life was not in my plans; however, His plans for us supersede our understanding as we fulfill His will on the earth. Not only did the gifts within me emerge in this ministry, but they were also sharpened, honed, and strengthened beyond measure. I am very grateful.

We embrace the will of God for our lives. We face the future without fear. We listen for His voice, His direction, and His instruction. Our hearts' desire is to be *"sons of God led by the Spirit of God"* (Romans 8:14, NIV) [paraphrased].

We embrace the truth that storms continue to blow throughout life.

We simply learned to fight!

We found the power within!

Summary

In summary, there are three reactions to the different storms of life. In the first type, we speak to the storm: "Peace, be still." The second type of storm requires a walk of faith with a faith action. We will hear God say, "Come up a little higher. Come. Follow Me." In the third type of storm, we hear, "Stand firm and declare *'It will be even as it was told me'*" (Acts 27:25, KJV). This is the most difficult storm. However, it is life-defining. Your ship may be lost, but your life will be saved; your destiny will be saved, and the purpose God ordained for you will be fulfilled. We found the following to be true:

"With every storm — we get stronger!"

Works Cited

Cerullo, Morris. <u>Proof Producers: "What We Must Do That We Might Work the Works of God."</u> (John 6:28, San Diego: Morris Cerullo World Evangelism 1998

Collins, Gary R. <u>How to Be a People Helper</u>. Wheaton: Tyndale House Publishers, Inc. 1995

Cole, Edwin Louis. <u>Maximized Manhood</u>. New Kensington: Whitaker House 2001

Copeland, Kenneth and Gloria. <u>From Faith to Faith: A Daily Guide to Victory</u>. Fort Worth: Kenneth Copeland Publications 1990

Eastman, Dick<u>. Change the World School of Prayer</u> Seminar/Notebook. Mission Hill: Change the World Ministries 1987

Gass, Bob and Debby. <u>The Word for You Today: Strength and Guidance for Daily</u>

<u>Living.</u> Alpharetta: Celebration, Inc. 2019 March 22 reference to John Ortberg

Lea, Larry. <u>Could You Not Tarry One Hour?</u> Altamonte Springs: Creation House 1987

Murdock, Mike. 101 Wisdom Keys. Dallas: Wisdom International 1994

Ortberg, John. The Life You've Always Wanted: Spiritual Disciplines for Ordinary People. Grand Rapids: Zondervan, 2002

Reader's Digest*Oxford Complete Wordfinder, Pleasantville: The Reader's Digest Association,

Inc. 1996

The Thompson Chain-Reference Bible New International Version, Compiled and Edited by

Frank Charles Thompson, D.D. Ph.D., Co-Published by The B. B. Kirkbride Bible Company, Inc. and The Zondervan Corporation 1983

The NIV/KJV Parallel Bible, The Zondervan Corporation 1983

The Amplified Bible, Expanded Edition, The Zondervan Corporation and The Lockman Foundation, 1987

The New King James Version, Thomas Nelson 1982

Willhite, B. J. Why Pray? Altamonte Springs: Creation House 1988

Willhite, B. J. with Dr. Judy Doyle. How Much Faith Does it Take to Move the Hand of God?

Rockwall: Church on the Rock Publication 1986